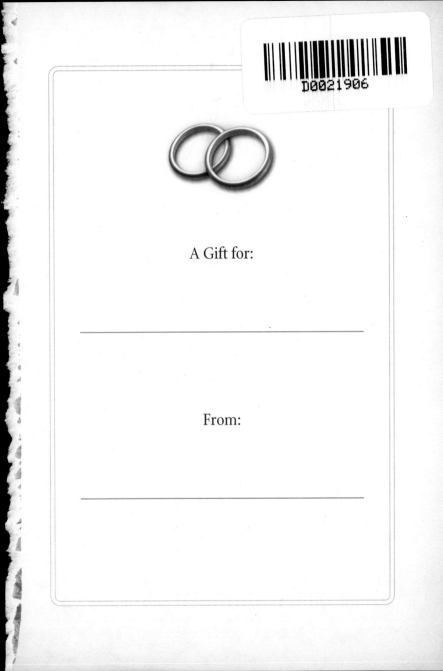

D0021906

A Gift for:

_____

From:

_____

Published in Nashville, Tennessee, by Thomas Nelson, Inc.

Published in association with the literary agency of Result Source, Inc., 3651 Peachtree Pkwy., Suite 330, Suwanee, GA 30024 and the Gibson Group, 2085 lakeshore Drl, Branson, MO 65616.

Project Editor: Pat Matuszak

Designed by Greg Jackson, Thinkpen Design, LLC

ISBN 13: 978-1-59145-567-7
ISBN 10: 1-59145-567-7

www.thomasnelson.com

Printed in China

I PROMISE
· CONSTITUTION ·

PREAMBLE: *When we wed I committed to love and cherish you all the days of my life, and I affirm that commitment today. I love you dearly, more than life itself. I honor you and place you above all other people in my life. My goal is to create in our marriage a place of safety and security in which you and I can share everything without fear and grow together in deeper love and intimacy. To confirm my commitment to this goal, I willingly make these five solemn promises to you.*

I PROMISE to conform my beliefs to God's truth. I will gain control of my outlook, emotions, and happiness by continually examining my deepest beliefs and striving to make them consistent with what God's Word says. I take sole responsibility for my beliefs with the understanding that they, not you, determine my emotions, expectations, and actions. Thus I lift from you the burden of being responsible for me.

I PROMISE to be filled by God. I will keep God in my heart as my source of joy and love. My love for you will be His love flowing through me. And I will receive your love as overflow from Him. I will base the security of our marriage on making Christ my boss. I will strive to conform to His image and follow all His commands, especially the one to love you and care for you all the days of my life.

I PROMISE to find God's best in every trial. I give you the security of knowing that the negative things that happen in our marriage will not destroy my love for you. I will not expect perfection from you, but will use even the irritations between us as opportunities to see my blind spots and foster my personal growth. I will call on the power of Christ to root out my weaknesses.

I PROMISE to listen and communicate with love. I will value every word you speak as a window to your heart. I will honor your opinions, feelings, needs, and beliefs so that you will feel free to speak honestly and openly with full security in my love for you. I will be open with you in communicating my heart and will consider your feelings and needs in all my words.

I PROMISE to serve you all the days of my life. I will fight all tendencies toward selfishness in me and focus on keeping you, your needs, and your goals before me at all times. I will serve you willingly and wholeheartedly, just as Christ served His disciples not only in small, humble ways but also by giving His life for them and for us as well.

DR. GARY SMALLEY

FIVE PROMISES
TO CREATE THE MARRIAGE
OF YOUR DREAMS

I
PROMISE
YOU

FOREVER

Published by
THOMAS NELSON
Since 1798

For other products and live events, visit us at:
www.thomasnelson.com

TABLE OF CONTENTS

FOREWORD:
PROMISES TO BUILD THE FOREVER KIND OF LOVE

How many "marriage books" have you been given or bought since you two became a couple? Whether you are newly weds with a freshly unwrapped stack of books or you have been married long enough to have a whole row of advice books in your bookcase, *I Promise You...Forever* will help you think in a new way about how to enhance your marriage.

In this book, Gary Smalley, America's foremost marriage expert, provides a revolutionary solution to the reason most marriage advice fails. His startling new conclusion: Great marriages are built on a foundation of trust, *not behavioral skills we learn to use.*

After counseling couples for many years, Dr. Smalley realized it's not enough to learn your partner's love language, be skilled in conflict resolution, control your emotions, or become an expert in the bedroom. Unless your spouse feels safe enough to open up his or her heart without fear of being judged, criticized, blamed, or rejected; nothing you do will be effective. It's only when couples feel emotionally "safe" that they can truly become one, as God intended. Based on 10 years of research, he shares heartfelt promises you can make to your mate that are guaranteed to build trust and help you both become the true soul mate, lover and friend you desire.

Security makes your marriage feel like the safest place on earth, the place where you want to live and grow and love. But to experience that level of security, you must build a sound relational security system and punch in the code to activate it just as you would with an electronic security system on your house. Then you'll be on your way to the best marriage you can imagine.

DR. GARY SMALLEY

The thirty promises in this book fall under 5 main commitments that Dr. Smalley determined were keys to having a love that lasts forever. The chart on the next page may be copied or cut out of the book to be posted where you will be most like to see it each day. Think about these thirty promises, a promise a day for thirty days, and see how they will change your marriage in a forever way.

THE MARRIAGE CONSTITUTION: AN AFFIRMATION OF LOVE

*M*arriage is an undertaking of untold importance. The home that lovers establish when they take their vows can affect all eternity. It is God's first earthly institution, the foundation of a stable society, and a source of untold potential for joy and fulfillment. So why shouldn't your marriage have a constitution?

I believe it should. That is why I have summarized the five main promises I've presented in this book and put them in the form of a constitution—the "I Promise" Constitution. You can adopt and sign the constitution as I have written it here or use it as a basis for creating your own. If you use mine, just cut it from the book and place it where you and your mate can look at it any time to remind yourselves of what you have committed to do in order to provide security for your marriage.

I PROMISE
· C O N S T I T U T I O N ·

PREAMBLE: *When we wed I committed to love and cherish you all the days of my life, and I affirm that commitment today. I love you dearly, more than life itself. I honor you and place you above all other people in my life. My goal is to create in our marriage a place of safety and security in which you and I can share everything without fear and grow together in deeper love and intimacy. To confirm my commitment to this goal, I willingly make these five solemn promises to you.*

I PROMISE to conform my beliefs to God's truth. I will gain control of my outlook, emotions, and happiness by continually examining my deepest beliefs and striving to make them consistent with what God's Word says. I take sole responsibility for my beliefs with the understanding that they, not you, determine my emotions, expectations, and actions. Thus I lift from you the burden of being responsible for me.

I PROMISE to be filled by God. I will keep God in my heart as my source of joy and love. My love for you will be His love flowing through me. And I will receive your love as overflow from Him. I will base the security of our marriage on making Christ my boss. I will strive to conform to His image and follow all His commands, especially the one to love you and care for you all the days of my life.

I PROMISE to find God's best in every trial. I give you the security of knowing that the negative things that happen in our marriage will not destroy my love for you. I will not expect perfection from you, but will use even the irritations between us as opportunities to see my blind spots and foster my personal growth. I will call on the power of Christ to root out my weaknesses.

I PROMISE to listen and communicate with love. I will value every word you speak as a window to your heart. I will honor your opinions, feelings, needs, and beliefs so that you will feel free to speak honestly and openly with full security in my love for you. I will be open with you in communicating my heart and will consider your feelings and needs in all my words.

I PROMISE to serve you all the days of my life. I will fight all tendencies toward selfishness in me and focus on keeping you, your needs, and your goals before me at all times. I will serve you willingly and wholeheartedly, just as Christ served His disciples not only in small, humble ways but also by giving His life for them and for us as well.

I PROMISE
TO CONFORM
MY BELIEFS TO
GOD'S TRUTH.

I will gain control of my outlook, emotions, and happiness by continually examining my deepest beliefs and striving to make them consistent with what God's Word says. I take sole responsibility for my beliefs with the understanding they, not you, determine my emotions, expectations, and actions. Thus I lift from you the burden of being responsible for me.

My goal is to create in our marriage a place of safety and security in which you and I can share everything without fear and grow together in deeper love and intimacy.

I PROMISE
TO HONOR
YOU.

Honor is a way of accurately seeing the immense value of a person made in God's image. God created each one of us as a one-of-a-kind person with unique gifts and a unique personality. He sees each of us as precious and valuable because He sees the innate worth He built into us.

Honor is so simple. It means to value another person highly as extremely important and of great worth. If you want that in the form of a definition, the one I prefer is "to give preference to others by attaching high value to them." A person who is highly honored will be thought of as a cherished treasure and treated with the kind of respect we give to royalty.

If you choose to look only at your mate's shortcomings, he or she may not seem to deserve honor. But that has nothing to do with it. Honor is not earned; it's a gift. It isn't purchased by your mate's actions or contingent on your own emotions. You give honor because you choose to give it, whether or not it's deserved. It's a decision you make.

I PROMISE TO ALWAYS REMEMBER OUR FIRST LOVE.

When God brought to Adam the newly created Eve, can you imagine what he thought? *Wow! When God said He'd give me a companion, never in my wildest dreams did I imagine anything like this. Man, what a treasure*!

Now, think back. Didn't you feel the same way when you married your mate? Didn't it feel as if you had discovered a cave filled with priceless gold, silver, diamonds, and sparkling gemstones? And it was true. When you married, you received a treasure of unfathomable worth. Maintaining that wonder is critically important, because it means you are still finding in your husband or wife reasons for honor.

I PROMISE TO REMEMBER YOU ARE GOD'S GIFT TO ME.

Picture your mate as personally autographed by God. Wouldn't you feel thrilled to be seen with someone who bore God's personal autograph? Wouldn't you want to have your picture taken with such a person and hang it in a prominent place?

When you look for the good and the honorable in your mate, you will find it. God instilled His glory into each of us.

C.S. Lewis reminded us that the original glory is lying just beneath the surface of every human. He said we must "...remember that the dullest and most uninteresting person you can talk to may one day be a creature which, if you saw it now, you would be strongly tempted to worship."

I PROMISE TO CHOOSE TO HONOR YOU OUTSIDE OF MY EMOTIONAL CLIMATE.

Our feelings always follow our beliefs and thoughts. Make the decision to treat your mate as a 100-carat diamond and your positive feelings for him or her will increase.

Regardless of what we believe about someone, whether positive or negative, we will find evidence to support that belief. This can have a major impact on your relationship. If you do not see your mate as a priceless treasure, you will tend to focus on negative actions as evidence of low worth and treat your mate accordingly. But if you choose to see your mate as a wonderful treasure, you will focus on his or her positive behavior as evidence of high worth. Both the positive and the negative are always there. Which you focus on is your choice.

Choosing to notice your mate's positive behavior is what the Apostle Paul said to do: "Finally, brethren, whatever is true, whatever is honorable, whatever is right, whatever is pure, whatever is lovely, whatever is of good repute, if there is any excellence and if anything worthy of praise, dwell on these things" (Philippians 4:8 NASB). Think of the good qualities of your mate and the happy surprise is that your feelings of affection will grow by leaps and bounds. When this happens, honor flows easily.

I PROMISE TO INSTALL AN EMOTIONAL SECURITY SYSTEM FOR OUR MARRIAGE.

Security is the unsung need, the overlooked ingredient that can make your marriage the best on the face of the earth. Security underscores and supports every facet of your relationship.

What I'm talking about here is emotional security—the security to truly open up and be known at a deep, intimate level without fear of being blamed, criticized, judged, or condemned.

Security makes your marriage feel like the safest place on earth, the place where you want to live and grow and love. But to experience that level of security, you must build a sound relational security system and punch in the code to activate it just as you would with an electronic security system on your house. Then you'll be on your way to the best marriage you can imagine.

I PROMISE
TO BE FILLED
BY GOD.

I will keep God in my heart as my source of joy and love. My love for you will be His love flowing through me. And I will receive your love as overflow from Him. I will base the security of our marriage on making Christ my boss. I will strive to conform to His image and follow all His commands, especially the one to love you and care for you all the days of my life. (Ephesians 5:25, 2 Corinthians 3:18)

I PROMISE
TO BE
FAITHFUL.

Promising to commit to God provides security for your mate. It gives your marriage a solid foundation by providing a transcendent source of authority under which both of you live.

A person committed to God is sensitive to His will, His rules, His design for relationships, behavior, and ethics. Promising to submit to God's authority assures your mate that you will not be guided by your own wants and whims. It means that in your treatment of the other you will be guided by solid, unchanging, biblical absolutes rather than your desires of the moment or by the fluctuating standards of a relativistic society.

When disagreements occur, you are committed to seeking the truth in a loving, open, and considerate way rather than resorting to your own subjective standards. When your mate sees that you are following God's rules for love and life rather than making them up as you go, he or she will feel much more relaxed, *more secure and safe* knowing you are committed to a power higher than yourself. Promising to put God at the foundation of your marriage provides the most solid security possible.

I PROMISE
TO LOVE YOU
UNCONDITIONALLY.

What is the secret to building the kind of marriage God wants for you? Unconditionally love without criticism or expectation. It's the hardest kind of love to give, but the one that brings all the blessings you can hold.

Would you like one good reason why you should love that blundering, frustrating, badly flawed spouse of yours unconditionally? It's simple...*because he or she needs it*. When a baby is born, we love that child because he needs it. When people are starving, we feed them because they are hungry. And that's the reason Jesus expressed His unconditional love for us on the cross . . . because we needed it. As He said, even "sinners" love the people who love them. The real test is how well we love someone who does not love us well. That is the true calling of Christ (Luke 6:32-35). A safe marriage is one in which each partner loves the other simply because he or she needs it.

I PROMISE TO MAKE JESUS THE SOURCE OF MY HAPPINESS AND STRENGTH.

For a boat, or anything electrical to function as it was designed, it needs to be connected to a power source. If human relationships are to function as they were designed, they too need to be connected to a power source. It's as if you have a built-in battery that needs daily charges to keep you feeling complete and satisfied.

For a long time I believed that I could keep that battery charged if I just plugged a 110-volt electrical cord into other people or my wife. Many of us enter marriage looking to our mate as the source of that power charge. We think, "Now that I have this person in my life, I am really going to have my needs met and be happy." We ultimately find, however, that our mates cannot recharge our battery. Our mates can be tremendous sources of help and encouragement, but if we expect them to be the source of our happiness, they are sure to disappoint us in the long run.

Since God made you for a relationship with Himself, the best thing you can ever do for yourself—and for your marriage—is to promise your mate that you will develop your personal connection to God through a dynamic faith in Christ.

I PROMISE
TO HAVE
GOD'S GOAL
FOR OUR
MARRIAGE.

It may surprise you to hear that God did not design marriage as a place where we can get all our needs met. In fact, nowhere does He tell us that happiness, a soul mate, companionship, sex, or even love is the purpose of marriage. He created it with something far more wonderful in mind.

God uses marriage to accomplish His primary goal for all Christians. The apostle Paul explained this goal; it is for us is to be *"conformed to the image of His Son"* (Rom 8:29). Becoming like Christ is God's primary goal for all Christians. Of course, you and I were originally created in God's image, but Adam and Eve messed that up for us. Now we get to spend the rest of our lives being transformed back into His image. And marriage is one of the best tools that He uses to accomplish that.

Therefore, as we evaluate our success in a marriage our focus should not be on whether our needs are being met. Instead, we must ask, *"Am I demonstrating the image and character of Jesus Christ?"*

I PROMISE
NOT TO "COAST"
IN OUR
RELATIONSHIP.

You cannot coast along and expect secure oneness to happen from romantic feelings and preconceived expectations.

You must consciously design your lives together to achieve oneness with Christ and each other. The world will work against you, and Satan will work against you. But the oneness you achieve with each other by growing closer to God will give you security that neither the world nor Satan can breach. Here are a few simple activities that will help couples grow toward this kind of oneness:

- Pray for each other
- Pray together
- Attend church together
- Serve in some type of church or mission service together
- Eat meals together
- Read the Bible together
- Discuss together what you are learning in your quiet time
- Scripture memorization together
- Attend a small group with other couples designed to help you grow closer together as a couple and with God

I PROMISE
TO FIND
GOD'S BEST
IN EVERY
TRIAL.

I give you the security of knowing that the negative things that happen in our marriage will not destroy my love for you. I will not expect perfection from you, but will use even the irritations between us as opportunities to see my blind spots and foster my personal growth. I will call on the power of Christ to root out my weaknesses. (Romans 8:28, James 1:12, Romans 5:3-5)

I PROMISE
TO FORGIVE.

When unresolved irritations cause damage to our relationships, one step is necessary before the relationship can resume, and that is forgiveness. Forgiveness is crucial to maintaining a marriage.

Forgiveness opens the door to repair and reestablishes security. When mates forgive they show their commitment to remaining connected. Therefore, one of the best promises you can make is that you will always be quick to seek forgiveness and quick to forgive. Without forgiveness you're not likely to make it to your fifth wedding anniversary, much less to your fiftieth.

What makes forgiveness so important? Well, aside from the impossibility of maintaining a marriage without it, forgiveness makes us more like God. It also improves our physical and emotional health. And it keeps security alive and well.

"Be kind to one another, tenderhearted, forgiving one another, even as God in Christ forgave you" (Ephesians 4:31-32). Forgiveness is for your own good.

I PROMISE NOT TO "FIX" YOU.

Sometimes we get bent out of shape over a very minor fault in our mate while harboring in our own life a major fault that we ignore. Jesus noted this tendency when He said:

"Do not judge so that you will not be judged. For in the way you judge, you will be judged; and by your standard of measure, it will be measured to you.

Why do you look at the speck that is in your brother's eye, but do not notice the log that is in your own eye? Or how can you say to your brother, 'Let me take the speck out of your eye,' and behold, the log is in your own eye? You hypocrite, first take the log out of your own eye, and then you will see clearly to take the speck out of your brother's eye" (Matthew 7:1-5 NASB).

Jesus knew us pretty well, didn't He? You see a little speck of sawdust (like smacking gum) in your mate's eye and it bugs you to no end. You make it your job to get that thing out of there. But all the while you have this big plank, or maybe even enormous logs stuck in your own eye, and you don't even notice them. Do you know what else I think Jesus was telling us? "You have enough logs in your own eye to keep both you and Me busy. Let's just work on changing you until you look more like Me. That'll take at least one lifetime."

I PROMISE TO MAKE OUR HOME A "JUDGMENT-FREE ZONE."

Looking at the logs in your own eye before removing the speck from your mate's eye is highly critical to the wellbeing of your marriage. And the reason is quite simple: judgment destroys security.

The mate who is always having his or her eyes examined for specks will have the sense of being under constant scrutiny. He or she will feel pressure to measure up in order to keep the love of the other. The message is, "If you want me to continue loving you, you'd better get rid of that irritating habit." This does not express unconditional love, and it's hardly the way to create security in a marriage. Security comes from knowing your mate will love you regardless of your flaws and shortcomings. Real love is unconditional.

If love is unconditional, there's no need for judgment. That's why James challenges Christians to conduct all their relationships in "judgment-free zones" in James 4:11-12.

I PROMISE
TO TAKE
RESPONSIBILITY
FOR MY
EMOTIONS.

"Therefore if you bring your gift to the altar, and there remember that your brother has something against you, leave your gift there before the altar, and go your way. First be reconciled to your brother, and then come and offer your gift" (Matthew 5:23-24). Our worship to God is meaningless until we make sure that people we have offended, or people we've been offended by, are freed from the bondage of anger, vengeance, or hate. When we free them we free ourselves.

If you're on the verge of being angry all the time, and your mate or your family has to tiptoe around as if stepping through a mine field, wondering which misstep will set off an explosion, you are doing them a great disservice. You may believe that what they do is the cause of your anger. But that is dead wrong. Your anger comes from inside you. Blaming your mate or your family for your anger makes them falsely responsible for it and allows you to evade responsibility that should be yours alone.

It's your own beliefs and thoughts that provoke your anger—not the actions of people around you. You need to sit down with them and say, "Look, I've been really angry with all of you. I blamed you for it. But I've learned it has nothing to do with you. My anger came from myself—from my own thoughts and beliefs. You were just an excuse for me to pull the trigger. I take full responsibility. I am so sorry that I've made you live in this minefield."

I PROMISE
TO FOCUS ON
YOUR VALUE
INSTEAD OF
WEAKNESSES.

Promise your mate that you will accept all the negative things that happen to you as opportunities for personal growth.

Promise that you will use both the little irritations that are inevitable in every marriage, as well as the major traumatic hurts and suffering to learn about yourself and discover your blind spots. Promise that once you identify these blind spots you will call on the power of Christ to root them out.

Promise this dear person in your life that your love is stronger than his or her faults. He is a treasure you will honor and love in spite of his faults. She is more precious to you than anything in your life, even if she does have a few flaws. Therefore you will always focus on your mate's value instead of weaknesses.

And in the words of Jesus himself, "Where your treasure is, there your heart will be also" (Matthew 6:21). You decide what is valuable to you, and your emotions will fall in line and validate that choice.

I PROMISE TO LISTEN AND COMMUNICATE WITH LOVE.

I will value every word you speak as a window to your heart. I will honor your opinions, feelings, needs, and beliefs so that you will feel free to speak honestly and openly with full security in my love for you. I will be open with you in communicating my heart and will consider your feelings and needs in all my words. (Ephesians 4:29)

I PROMISE
TO LISTEN.

James 1:19 says if you're quick to listen, you'll be slow to anger. And "quick to listen" doesn't mean you should get the listening over with as fast as you can. It means slow down and listen until you understand. And understanding tends to displace anger.

The bulk of the man's communication is in pursuit of his competitive goals. The bulk of the woman's is in pursuit of relationships. So in a sense, men and women live in two different worlds. When they marry and begin to build a shared world of their own, the two worlds they come out of can either collide or blend. More often than not, there's quite a bit of colliding before the blending begins as both sexes naively assume the other communicates in much the same way as they do. While men and women come from different worlds, both need to be accepted, understood, and valued for who they are as God has created them. Neither sex should selfishly expect to understand the other solely on its own terms.

I PROMISE
TO GIVE
YOU TLC.

We consistently underestimate it, undersell it, undervalue it, and under use it. Yet touch has the power to calm, reassure, transfer courage, and stabilize a situation spinning out of control.

When we touch our mates lovingly, we push back the threatening shadows of bitterness, loneliness, and insecurity. A loving touch can immediately drain anger from a situation. A gentle touch says, "You are valuable to me."

The proven power of touch is amazing. Medical studies show that men who meaningfully hug and touch others stay healthier and live longer. Research from Dr. Allan Shore of the UCLA School of Medicine shows that when babies aren't touched in their first two months, they can suffer permanent brain damage. Many children in understaffed orphanages die if they don't get touched. Would you like to lower your mate's blood pressure, improve your high school student's brain function, or protect your grade-school children from involvement in an immoral relationship later in life? Would you like to add up to two years to your own life? Findings in recent scientific studies show that touch can actually provide all these benefits. We give the people we care about an incredible gift when we reach out and touch them. The UCLA studies found that to maintain emotional and physical health, men and women need eight to ten meaningful touches every day.

I PROMISE
TO LISTEN TO
YOU THROUGH
THE FILTER OF
GOD'S LOVE.

All the jokes seem to be about men not understanding women, but in fact, it works both ways. The reason is that the innate differences between men and women result in different approaches and different ways of communicating. Therefore, each sex goes at the relationship in an altogether different way.

Most men focus on the marriage as a thing to be built, maintained, and defended. He is the hunter/farmer. He goes out and applies his brain or brawn to wrest the needs of his home from a hostile world. When he comes home he's in his castle, his haven of rest, walled off and insulated from the threats and dangers he's fought all day. Most women focus on the marriage in terms of emotional connection. She too wants the home to be a protected haven, but for her it's one where intimate relationships can flourish. She finds her greatest security in an intimate connection with the heart of her husband.

Thus, for the most part, men and women have different needs, which they hope the marriage will satisfy. Men, the competitors, the mighty hunters, feel a need to be admired. Women, the nesters and nurturers, feel a need for emotional intimacy and security. They attempt to make this connection by communicating.

I PROMISE
TO RESPECT OUR
DIFFERENCES.

We men don't need to become feminized, but
we do need to move toward women in the area of
communication and understanding. Talking to
our wives will not make us less macho. Meeting a
woman's needs is the epitome of masculinity. At the
same time women need to remember that men do
not share their need to talk, and understand that
masculine silence does not indicate a lack of love.

Time, education, and insight can give a man more understanding of women, but to expect him to enter marriage with the same relational approaches as women is expecting a dog to purr like a kitten. Each mate, by learning more of the nature and language of the other, can achieve great communication in marriage. And effective communication will double your marital satisfaction. Effective communication will make your marriage more intimate and peaceful and eliminate most of your escalated arguments. Expressing your feelings gives your mate a better understanding of your primary needs. The better you understand each other's primary needs—those mystifying mysteries that each of you brings from the masculine and feminine worlds—the deeper you can go into true intimacy.

I PROMISE TO WORK WITH YOU FOR A WIN-WIN SOLUTION TO OUR DIFFERENCES.

I want to do a lot of things, but I can't just do whatever I want because I'm married to a person who has beliefs, needs, and feelings of her own. We love each other and neither wants the other to feel trampled on.

So we operate by this rule: When we disagree, we don't move forward until both of us feel good about the solution. When my wife says to me, "I don't want to move forward until you're happy," I relax. She doesn't want me to lose. And because I love my wife, I don't want her to lose either. We use these three steps:

1. We communicate honestly and without judgment. We listen to the other's feelings, needs, and beliefs, and openly communicate ours. We don't try to change or pressure each other. We listen for the heart beneath the words.

2. We place on the table ideas and alternatives, discussing their pros and cons and testing each for acceptability to the other.

3. We find solutions that both partners like.

I PROMISE
TO SERVE YOU
ALL THE DAYS
OF MY LIFE.

I will fight all tendencies toward selfishness in me and focus on keeping you, your needs, and your goals before me at all times. I will serve you willingly and wholeheartedly just as Christ served His disciples not only in small, humble ways but also by giving His life for them and for us as well. (Galatians 5:13)

I PROMISE TO PROVIDE FOR YOU.

Once we adopt the attitude that we are here to serve, just as Christ was, it will affect all areas of our lives.

Paul lays upon husbands a huge responsibility toward their wives in Ephesians 5. Look at some of his words: "Husbands ought to love their wives as they love their own bodies....No one hates his own body but lovingly cares for it" "Each man must love his wife as he loves himself." And most important: "And you husbands must love your wives with the same love Christ showed the church. He gave up his life for her to make her holy and clean..."

The Bible seems to give us men the greater responsibility toward serving and caring for our wives. They serve us to the point of submitting, but we serve them to the point of dying.

I PROMISE TO PUT YOUR NEEDS ABOVE MY OWN.

Being a servant in marriage is putting your mate first—even above yourself—and giving yourself for the other.

For Christ this meant dying for others, and in some rare cases it may mean that in a marriage. But love seldom requires a once-and-for-all sacrifice of life or limb. Usually the giving of yourself is an ongoing thing, a continuing attitude that looks perpetually to the welfare of your mate. It's saying, "I promise to make you more important than me. I promise to put your needs above my own. I promise to give up my preferences and even my needs if it serves your wellbeing."

I can assure you that my happiest times have always been those in which I was clearly adopting the attitude of a servant. I'm not being a servant if I expect anything in return—even appreciation.

I PROMISE TO FOLLOW JESUS AS MY MENTOR.

Jesus is the perfect mentor for developing a life that serves our mate and others. He was the Lord of the universe, but He showed in His life that the highest calling of a great leader is to be a servant.

Luke 22:24 shows His disciples caught up in their own ambition for success and power, arguing over who would be the greatest in the coming kingdom. But Jesus rebuked them saying, "Those who are the greatest should take the lowest rank, and the leader should be like a servant. Normally the master sits at the table and is served by his servants. But not here! For I am your servant."

Jesus was telling them that true leadership is not insisting on being the one in charge, making all the decisions, and determined to rule the roost. A true leader looks to the needs of others and sees that they are met. When I grow up I want to be a leader like my big brother Jesus. I want to be known as a servant.

What do you look like when you become like Jesus? The picture that always comes to my mind is that of Him wearing a towel, bending over the dirty feet of those twelve dear friends, washing away the grime of the road. We become most like Christ when we serve others.

The apostle Paul said, "Husbands love your wives, just as Christ also loved the church and gave Himself up for her" (Ephesians 5:25 NASB). That is ultimate servanthood, and marriage provides the ideal environment for exercising it.

I PROMISE
TO LEARN
WHAT YOUR
NEEDS ARE.

Do you really know your mate? Have you managed to put aside your own rights so you can focus on what makes your husband or wife tick? Have you made it your goal to study your mate to know the innermost desires and needs in his or her heart?

To be a servant in marriage you must know your spouse. Genuine serving means learning to identify your husband's or wife's specific needs and looking for creative ways to meet them.

I stress the need for each to learn the other's needs, because it's all too easy to assume that your mate's needs are the same as your own. When this happens you may plunge in all gung-ho with good intentions of serving yet fail to meet the true needs of your mate's heart. Our normal habit is to see things from our own perspective with little understanding of the viewpoint of others. To be a genuine servant, you must know your mate's heart.

How do you discover what your mate's needs are? Well, you might consider just asking. Sometimes we make things more complex than they need to be. If you want information, asking and listening is often the simplest and most effective way to get it.

I PROMISE TO MAKE MY ULTIMATE GOAL TO BECOME CHRIST'S SERVANT.

If you want a happy marriage, the best way to get there is to not make a happy marriage your ultimate goal, but simply to become more like Christ. He was a servant, and He said that the greatest people are those who choose to be servants like Him. Serve your mate selflessly, and you will find happiness in marriage. And what's more *secure* in a marriage than to have a mate whose ultimate goal is to become Christ's servant, which means that your mate will love you unconditionally? That's why my goal in marriage is no longer to be a great husband; it's to be a great servant. Great servants make great marriages.